TABLE OF CONTEN

100 AI Tools for University Students

A. Writing & Essay Assistance

Grammarly
Helps correct grammar, spelling, clarity, and tone issues.
Free basic version, Paid premium version.
Website: grammarly.com

QuillBot
Paraphrases sentences, summarizes articles, helps in citations.
Free basic use, Paid for full features.
Website: quillbot.com

Hemingway Editor
Improves readability, detects passive voice and complex sentences.
Free online version, Paid for desktop app.
Website: hemingwayapp.com

Wordtune
AI tool that rephrases and enhances sentences.
Free basic plan, Paid premium plan.
Website: wordtune.com

Jasper
Writes essays, blog posts, creative writing based on input prompts.
Paid (offers a free trial).
Website: jasper.ai

SudoWrite
Assists in expanding and creatively writing essays or stories.
Paid (with trial available).
Website: sudowrite.com

Writesonic
Generates essays, blog posts, ad copies quickly.
Free trial, Paid plans.
Website: writesonic.com

Rytr
Affordable AI writer for short articles and essays.
Free basic account, Paid for unlimited usage.
Website: rytr.me

HyperWrite
Gives smart suggestions while writing essays or reports.
Free limited version, Paid plan available.
Website: hyperwriteai.com

Copy.ai
Generates ideas, outlines, and even parts of essays.
Free basic, Paid premium plans.
Website: copy.ai

INK Editor
Optimizes essays for SEO and better readability.
Free trial, Paid versions.
Website: inkforall.com

AI Dungeon
Generates creative storytelling and adventure narratives.
Free with limited access, Paid for unlimited adventures.
Website: aidungeon.io

Paragraph AI
Drafts essays, emails, or LinkedIn posts instantly.
Free limited, Paid subscription.
Website: paragraphai.com

Shortly AI
Focuses on long-form writing like essays and assignments.
Paid.
Website: shortlyai.com

Slick Write
Grammar checker that detects potential stylistic errors.
Free.
Website: slickwrite.com

Outwrite
Helps rewrite sentences, improves grammar, and clarity.
Free limited, Paid premium plan.
Website: outwrite.com

Paperpal
Gives instant feedback for academic writing.
Free limited version, Paid full access.
Website: paperpal.com

Compose AI
An AI Chrome extension that predicts and writes emails, essays.
Free basic, Paid plans.
Website: compose.ai

Jenni AI
AI assistant to help draft essays and
academic papers quickly.
Free trial, Paid subscriptions.
Website: jenni.ai

Trinka
Academic writing grammar checker for
technical writing.
Free trial, Paid versions.
Website: trinka.ai

B. Research & Learning

Elicit
Finds relevant academic papers and
suggests research directions.
Free.
Website: elicit.org

Perplexity AI
An AI search engine that summarizes
research fast.
Free.
Website: perplexity.ai

Research Rabbit
Tracks academic research and suggests related papers.
Free.
Website: researchrabbitapp.com

Connected Papers
Builds a network map of related academic papers.
Free.
Website: connectedpapers.com

Consensus
Summarizes findings from multiple
research papers.
Free.
Website: consensus.app

Scite.ai
Helps verify scientific claims with
citations and research.
Paid with free trial.
Website: scite.ai

Semantic Scholar
Search millions of research papers for free.
Free.
Website: semanticscholar.org

Paperpile
Organizes research papers and references easily.
Paid.
Website: paperpile.com

Zotero
Free tool for collecting, organizing, and citing research.
Free.
Website: zotero.org

EndNote
Advanced reference manager for researchers.
Paid.
Website: endnote.com

ReadPaper
AI summarizer for lengthy academic papers.
Free.
Website: readpaper.com

Scholarcy
Summarizes long academic papers into key points.
Paid (with trial).
Website: scholarcy.com

Mendeley
Reference manager and academic
social network.
Free.
Website: mendeley.com

Iris.ai
Helps students find and digest academic
papers.
Paid with academic discount.
Website: iris.ai

Litmaps
Visual maps showing how papers are connected.
Free limited, Paid full.
Website: litmaps.com

Explainpaper
Explains hard-to-understand academic papers easily.
Free.
Website: explainpaper.com

SciSpace
Simplifies academic papers and helps
with writing.
Free limited, Paid options.
Website: scispace.com

DeepL Write
Provides professional quality rewrites
and translations.
Free.
Website: deepl.com/write

CiteThisForMe
Quickly generates citations in multiple formats.
Free.
Website: citethisforme.com

Flowcite
All-in-one academic writing and citation tool.
Free limited, Paid premium.
Website: flowcite.com

C. Study Aids & Note-Taking

Notion AI
AI-powered note-taking, task management, and study planning.
Free personal plan, Paid premium.
Website: notion.so

Evernote
Organizes notes, tasks, and schedules.
Free basic plan, Paid plans.
Website: evernote.com

Otter.ai
Records and transcribes lectures and
meetings automatically.
Free basic, Paid premium.
Website: otter.ai

Fireflies.ai
Meeting and lecture transcription service
with summaries.
Free limited, Paid full features.
Website: fireflies.ai

Reflect Notes
Linked note-taking for deeper study thinking.
Paid (with free trial).
Website: reflect.app

Obsidian
Powerful knowledge base for students using linked notes.
Free, Paid sync service optional.
Website: obsidian.md

Tana
Note-taking tool designed for networked thinking.
Free (beta access).
Website: tana.inc

Cogram
AI that takes notes during meetings automatically.
Paid.
Website: cogram.com

Mem.ai
Smart note-taking app that organizes thoughts automatically.
Free basic, Paid plans.
Website: mem.ai

Supernormal
Automated meeting note recorder with AI summaries.
Free limited, Paid full version.
Website: supernormal.com

D. Presentation & Design Tools

Beautiful.ai
Create stunning, smart presentations automatically.
Free trial, Paid plans.
Website: beautiful.ai

Tome
AI storytelling platform for slide creation and portfolio work.
Free with paid upgrade.
Website: tome.app

Gamma.app
Create presentations, documents, and webpages instantly.
Free basic, Paid full options.
Website: gamma.app

Canva AI
Design posters, social media posts, and slides easily.
Free basic, Paid Canva Pro.
Website: canva.com

Visme
Presentation and infographic builder with templates.
Free basic access, Paid plans.
Website: visme.co

Simplified
Graphic design and AI writing tools for students.
Free with Paid options.
Website: simplified.com

Designs.ai
Create logos, videos, banners with AI help.
Paid (offers free trials).
Website: designs.ai

Decktopus
Quickly create professional AI-generated presentations.
Free limited, Paid upgrades.
Website: decktopus.com

Kroma.ai
Ready-made pitch decks and
presentation templates.
Paid.
Website: kroma.ai

Presentations.AI
Smart AI tool for university presentation
creation.
Paid.
Website: presentations.ai

E. Creativity & Brainstorming

Midjourney
Generates artistic visuals for projects and presentations.
Paid (with trial use on Discord).
Website: midjourney.com

DALL·E 3 (OpenAI)
Create images from text prompts.
Free limited (through ChatGPT Plus).
Website: openai.com/dall-e

Craiyon
Free image generator based on AI prompts.
Free.
Website: craiyon.com

Runway ML
Generates videos, edits images with AI.
Free basic, Paid premium features.
Website: runwayml.com

NightCafe Creator
Make AI-generated artworks for study projects.
Free limited, Paid for credits.
Website: nightcafe.studio

Dream by Wombo
AI app that turns your text into art.
Free basic, Paid premium.
Website: dream.ai

PromptHero
Get the best prompts for creative AI
tools.
Free.
Website: prompthero.com

Magenta Studio
Create music with AI if you study
arts/music.
Free.
Website: magenta.tensorflow.org/studio

]

Soundraw.io
Generate music based on mood or theme instantly.
Paid.
Website: soundraw.io

Boomy
Create and release original music in minutes.
Free limited, Paid upgrades.
Website: boomy.com

F. Focus & Productivity Boosters

Forest App
Stay focused by planting virtual trees.
Paid app.
Website: forestapp.cc

Focusmate
Virtual body doubling to boost study sessions.
Free 3 sessions/week, Paid unlimited.
Website: focusmate.com

Serene
Simple planner combined with focus
mode timer.
Paid.
Website: sereneapp.com

Motion
Automatically schedules tasks around
your calendar.
Paid.
Website: usemotion.com

Freedom.to
Blocks distracting websites and apps during study.
Paid (offers free trial).
Website: freedom.to

Cold Turkey
Extreme productivity tool that blocks distractions hard.
Paid (one-time).
Website: getcoldturkey.com

RescueTime
Tracks time spent studying vs.
distracted.
Free limited, Paid premium.
Website: rescuetime.com

Brain.fm
Music scientifically designed to improve
focus.
Paid (with trial).
Website: brain.fm

PomoDone
Pomodoro timer that connects with task managers.
Free basic, Paid features.
Website: pomodoneapp.com

Tide
Focus timer combined with relaxing sounds.
Free basic, Paid upgrades.
Website: tide.fm

G. Math & Coding Help

Wolfram Alpha
Answers math, science, and engineering questions instantly.
Free limited, Paid Pro.
Website: wolframalpha.com

Photomath
Scan math problems and get step-by-step explanations.
Free basic, Paid advanced solutions.
Website: photomath.com

Mathway
Solve math problems from algebra to calculus easily.
Free basic, Paid detailed steps.
Website: mathway.com

Symbolab
Advanced math calculator and solver.
Free limited, Paid full access.
Website: symbolab.com

Khan Academy
Free courses in math, science, coding.
Free.
Website: khanacademy.org

Codex by OpenAI
Helps write code faster from natural language.
Integrated inside platforms (like GitHub Copilot, Paid).
Website: openai.com

Replit
Online coding platform with AI coding assistant.
Free basic, Paid premium.
Website: replit.com

GitHub Copilot
Autocompletes code with AI suggestions.
Paid.
Website: github.com/features/copilot

Codeium
Free alternative to GitHub Copilot for
code suggestions.
Free.
Website: codeium.com

AskCodi
Code generation and auto-complete
assistant.
Free limited, Paid plans.
Website: askcodi.com

H. Career & Interview Preparation

Interview Warmup (by Google)
Practice common interview questions with AI feedback.
Free.
Website: grow.google/certificates/interview-warmup

VMock
Smart career readiness platform that reviews resumes.
Free through many universities, Paid otherwise.
Website: vmock.com

Resume.io
AI resume builder and templates.
Free limited, Paid premium.
Website: resume.io

Kickresume
Create resumes, cover letters, and portfolios.
Free limited, Paid plans.
Website: kickresume.com

Skillroads
AI resume and cover letter writer.
Paid.
Website: skillroads.com

Enhancv
Beautiful AI-generated resumes and
career advice.
Free limited, Paid full access.
Website: enhancv.com

LoopCV
Automates job applications to multiple companies.
Free basic, Paid plans.
Website: loopcv.pro

Hiration
Career platform for AI resumes and interview prep.
Paid.
Website: hiration.com

Teal HQ
Career and job tracking platform with AI help.
Free with Paid options.
Website: tealhq.com

Jobscan
Optimize resumes based on job descriptions using AI.
Free limited scans, Paid unlimited.
Website: jobscan.co